ESSENTIAL CONCEPTS IN COMPUTER SCIENCE

THE POSITIVE AND NEGATIVE IMPACTS OF COMPUTERS IN SOCIETY

DANIEL R. FAUST

PowerKiDS press.
New York

Published in 2019 by The Rosen Publishing Group, Inc.
29 East 21st Street, New York, NY 10010

First Edition

Editor: Jane Katirgis
Book Design: Reann Nye

Photo Credits: Cover Umberto Shtanzman/Shutterstock.com; pp. 5, 19 Rawpixel.com/Shutterstock.com; pp. 7, 13 Syda Productions/Shutterstock.com; pp. 8, 10 LightField Studios/Shutterstock.com; p. 9 pathdoc/Shutterstock.com; p. 11 espies/Shutterstock.com; p. 15 Joe Raedle/Getty Images North America/Getty Images; p. 17 Ulrike Schmitt-Hartmann/Taxi/Getty Images; pp. 21, 29 Monkey Business Images/Shutterstock.com; p. 23 NadyaEugene/Shutterstock.com; pp. 24, 27, 30 wavebreakmedia/Shutterstock.com; p. 25 PeopleImages/E+/Getty Images.

Library of Congress Cataloging-in-Publication Data

Names: Faust, Daniel R., author.
Title: The positive and negative impacts of computers in society / Daniel R. Faust.
Description: New York : PowerKids Press, [2019] | Series: Essential concepts in computer science | Includes bibliographical references and index.
Identifiers: LCCN 2017054345| ISBN 9781538331699 (library bound) | ISBN 9781538331705 (pbk.) | ISBN 9781538331712 (6 pack)
Subjects: LCSH: Internet–Social aspects–Juvenile literature. | Computers–Social aspects–Juvenile literature. | Information technology–Social aspects–Juvenile literature.
Classification: LCC HM851 .F38 2019 | DDC 302.23/1–dc23
LC record available at https://lccn.loc.gov/2017054345

Manufactured in the United States of America

CPSIA Compliance Information: Batch #CS18PK: For Further Information contact Rosen Publishing, New York, New York at 1-800-237-9932

CONTENTS

EARLY COMPUTERS

Have you used a computer today? You probably use computers at home and at school. Your parents probably use computers at work.

The earliest computers were giant machines used by governments, universities, and the military. These computers took up entire rooms. The first personal computers were expensive. As technology advanced, computers became cheaper and easier to **manufacture**. More people were able to afford them.

Today's computers are small enough to fit on a desk or carry in a pocket. They make our lives simpler by doing many positive things. Need to do some quick shopping, write a report, or organize music and photos? A computer can handle these tasks easily. People are also able to work from home and sell things easily on the Internet. But there are negative sides to computer use, too. They include cyberbullying, computer addiction, and hacking.

COMPUTER CONNECTION

The earliest home computers were do-it-yourself kits that had to be assembled by the user. You can still buy computer kits if you think you want to build your own computer.

Computers make our lives easier at home and at school.

TODAY'S COMPUTER USE

Owning a computer used to be a luxury, but in the 21st century, computers have become common in the home, school, and office. Even our smartphones are basically handheld computers.

You and your friends probably use computers at school. When you need to find information for a homework assignment, you may do most of your research online. We use computers to play games, shop, and keep in touch with friends and family. Your parents use computers for a lot of the same things that you do. They also probably use computers to pay bills and manage a **budget**. Computers have also become a main way that a lot of people watch movies and television shows, read books, and listen to music.

COMPUTER CONNECTION

A modern smartphone has almost three times the processing power of a 1985 Cray-2 supercomputer. That means the phone in your parent's pocket is more powerful than a computer that was the size of a large kitchen appliance.

Many people carry a computer in their pocket at all times. In a world with smartphones, it is hard to believe computers once took up an entire room.

EMAIL, IMs, AND SOCIAL MEDIA

It wasn't too long ago that the only way to keep in touch with friends and family around the world was to make a phone call or send a letter. Computers changed all of that. Computers and the Internet have made it easier for people to stay in touch.

Imagine that your friend lives on the other side of town. You want to know if your friend wants to go to the

If you sent someone a handwritten letter, it might take them a month to reply. Email and texting allow us to communicate with other people almost instantly.

park and play baseball. You could walk to your friend's house to see if she's home. You could call her. Or you could just hop on a computer or smartphone and send your friend a quick message, asking if she'd like to meet you at the park. Maybe you have grandparents, aunts and uncles, or cousins who live in another country. Email, texts, messages sent over social media, and video chats allow you to keep in touch with relatives no matter how far away they live.

Perhaps the biggest change that has happened to communication during the digital age is the rise of social media. More than 60 percent of teenagers have at least one account on a site such as Facebook, Twitter, or Instagram. Social media gives young people the chance to keep in touch with friends and family, discover **peers** with similar interests, and express themselves through art, music, and the sharing of ideas. One of the greatest benefits of social media is that it allows teenagers to explore, develop, and express their individual identity.

There are a lot of social media sites on the Internet. These sites give you the chance to express yourself and learn how to interact with others.

THE RISE OF CYBERBULLYING

Bullying is nothing new. Kids and teenagers have been dealing with bullies for as long as anyone can remember. However, the Internet and the popularity of social media has given bullies a new tool. The same sites that you use to chat and share art and music with your friends can be turned against you.

Cyberbullying takes many different forms. Cyberbullies can send mean or abusive text messages or emails. They might post rumors on social media sites or spread embarrassing pictures or videos. Unlike regular bullying, cyberbullying does not end when the school day is over. It can happen any time, whether the victim is at home or in school. Cyberbullying can be done **anonymously** and can spread quickly to lots of people. It can be very hard to trace the source of cyberbullying.

If you are the victim of a cyberbully, do not respond. Save the message and show it to an adult you trust.

MAKING THE WORLD SMALLER

Computers have done much more than just help keep friends and family connected. Computers have made it possible to connect with people from different countries and cultures. This is what people mean when they say that computers and the Internet have made the world smaller.

In the past, most people never knew much about the world beyond their home town. The digital age makes it easier for people to broaden their horizons. Interacting with people from other cultures is one way to better understand those cultures and fight **prejudice**. The Internet also allows us to watch news from around the world as it happens. Many social media sites allow users to post when they are safe during natural disasters and other tragedies.

ARAB SPRING

The Arab Spring was a wave of pro-democracy protests and uprisings that took place in the Middle East and North Africa during 2010 and 2011. These protests challenged the governments that were in power. Social media networks such as Twitter were used by Arab Spring movements to organize protests and to spread stories about the protests around the world.

Hurricane Harvey struck Texas in 2017 and caused massive flooding. Social media was used during this natural disaster to send news to the rest of the world.

HACKERS AND CYBERCRIME

Cybercrime might be the biggest threat we face in the digital age. It used to be extremely difficult for criminals to obtain people's personal data, such as credit card numbers and banking information. However, the more time we spend online, the easier it is for hackers and other cybercriminals to steal this information.

Criminals can **intercept** the information you send over the Internet whenever you shop online. They can spy on your activities without you knowing. Some hackers are talented enough to break into the computer systems used by banks and retail stores. They can then steal your personal data and credit card information.

HISTORY'S BIGGEST HACKS

Between 2005 and 2012, a group of Russian and Ukrainian hackers attacked a number of banks and corporations. They stole 160 million credit and debit card numbers and breached 800,000 bank accounts. In 2017, cybercriminals stole information from Equifax, a credit-reporting agency. Names, social security numbers, and birthdays of up to 143 million people were taken.

Connecting wirelessly to the Internet makes our lives easier, but using an unsecure Wi-Fi connection can make it easier for hackers to steal your personal information.

There are a number of different ways that cybercriminals operate. The most common tool used by cybercriminals is malware, short for malicious software. Cybercriminals use malware to infect other people's computers. There are many kinds of malware, and each kind behaves differently.

A computer worm is a type of malware that **replicates** itself and spreads to other computers. Some computer worms simply slow down the computers they infect. Others can carry viruses. A virus carried by

HACKER LINGO

ADWARE: Software that automatically downloads unwanted advertising materials, or ads.

BLACK HAT: A term for a hacker who breaks into computer systems for criminal means or personal gain.

PHISHING: Sending fake emails in an attempt to trick the receiver into revealing personal information.

SPAMMING: Sending unwanted emails in large quantities to multiple recipients.

WHITE HAT: A term for a hacker who breaks into systems to locate weaknesses or test security measures.

Hackers like to hide malware in pop-up ads. Never click on any links or pop-ups that you don't trust. It's better to be safe than sorry.

a computer worm is called a payload. Ransomware makes it impossible for victims to access their information unless they pay a ransom to the cybercriminal. Spyware is a type of malware that "spies" on the victim's computer activities. Spyware can allow a cybercriminal to capture a victim's username and password for a number of different sites, as well as banking or credit card information.

STAYING SAFE

Cyberbullies and hackers are not the only threat you might face online. For all of the benefits that computers have brought to society, it's important to remember to protect yourself. Luckily for you, staying safe in the digital age is easy as long as you use your head.

The easiest way to prevent hackers from getting your personal information is to avoid giving it out. Only enter your usernames and passwords on sites that you know are safe. Do not open files or click on any links that you receive in emails from unknown senders. Avoid clicking on pop-up ads, since this is how many cybercriminals infect computers with malware. It's also important to be aware of potential online predators. Never give your address or telephone number to a stranger you meet online.

COMPUTER CONNECTION

An online predator is an adult who uses the Internet to target children and teenagers. These criminals befriend their victims online in order to harm them in the real world.

Your parents probably have rules about being online. This may feel unfair, but these rules are your parents' way of keeping you safe.

COMPUTERS ON THE JOB

Computers and computer technology have had a huge impact on the modern workforce. Computers have changed the way people work. They make certain jobs easier through **automation**. Computers have also provided a new level of flexibility. Email, messaging, file transferring, and cloud computing all allow people to telecommute, or work remotely. This means someone can be employed by a company even if they are unable to physically travel to the job site. This also makes it easier for people to work as **freelancers**.

It is getting more and more difficult to find an industry that does not use computers in some way. Retail stores use computers to track inventory and place orders with distributors. Many retail stores have customer rewards programs for frequent shoppers. The customer's information is stored in a computer database.

COMPUTER CONNECTION

Working freelance is a great decision for many people. The hours are flexible and you get to be your own boss. However, freelance jobs can lack job security and benefits such as health insurance.

You used to have to move to big cities for certain kinds of jobs. Now, technology makes it possible for people to work from anywhere, even the beach!

Hotels and airlines use computerized systems to help customers book rooms or flights. Hospitals and clinics use computers to store patient records, as well as track the inventory of drugs and other medications. When you deposit money in a bank, that transaction is stored on the bank's computer servers. This allows customers to access that money at another bank or through online banking. It might be hard to believe, but even an industry such as

DATABASE ADMINISTRATOR

As computers became more common in the workplace, one occupation that saw immediate growth was the database administrator. Database administrators are in charge of making sure the servers that contain a company's business data and customer information are organized and efficient. The database administrator is also responsible for the safety and security of this sensitive data, making sure it is not lost or stolen.

The digital age has brought many changes. One change is the creation of jobs such as mobile app developer. Mobile app developers are responsible for creating the apps that run on your smartphone or tablet.

construction relies on computers. Construction companies use global positioning software and electronic **surveying** equipment. Computers also help construction companies generate cost estimates when planning a new job.

A CHANGING WORKPLACE

Computers have changed the way a lot of jobs are done. They have increased **precision** and efficiency in a number of industries. They have also created a number of jobs, such as software designers, database administrators, and computer technicians. However, there is a drawback to the increased use of computers in the workplace.

The introduction of computers in the workplace has created many high-skilled, high-paying jobs. However, many simpler jobs have been lost. In many places warehouse clerks and basic data processors have been replaced by computer

MAN VS. MACHINE

Fear of new technology in the workplace is nothing new. During the Industrial Revolution, workers on farms and in factories were replaced by machines that could do the work of several people. Hiring fewer workers meant business owners would earn more profit. A similar thing happened in the early 20th century when manufacturing and other industries began using robots.

Like other new technology, computers have made it possible for one or two workers to do the job of many, particularly in factories and warehouses.

automation. The debate over the drawbacks of computers in the workplace has become an issue of social class, as many of the jobs being replaced by computers belong to people from lower social classes who have less access to higher education.

COMPUTER ADDICTION

Are you addicted to your computer or the Internet? This may sound like a silly question, but as we spend more and more hours a day sitting in front of a computer, it's possible some people develop an unhealthy relationship with computers.

Computer addiction can take many forms. If you ignore daily routines or personal relationships in order to spend time on the computer, you might have a computer addiction. Computer addiction can lead to your shopping online or checking social media when you should be studying or working, or staying up all night playing computer games. If you think you might have a computer addiction, you can try limiting your computer use to a specific time of day or location. It's important to remember that it's always okay to ask for help.

COMPUTER CONNECTION

Fear of missing out, or FOMO, is a form of social anxiety where an individual feels the need to stay connected to social media because something more interesting might be happening somewhere else. FOMO is a result of the constant stream of information we receive from the Internet and social media.

Computers are an important part of many people's day-to-day lives, but there can be too much of a good thing. It is not healthy to spend too much time on the computer.

TAKING THE GOOD WITH THE BAD

Some people will tell you that computers are the greatest thing humanity has ever invented. Others will say that computers have destroyed society. Of course, neither of these statements is true. Like many things, computers and the changes they have brought to our lives are a mix of positive and negative.

Computers help us in many ways. They make it easier to communicate and do schoolwork. Computers keep us entertained by allowing us to stream music and movies or to play computer games. But computers have drawbacks, too. Computers can expose you to people who might want to steal your identity or cause you harm. The most important thing to remember is that computers, like any other tool, should be used responsibly.

GLOSSARY

anonymously: Done without revealing one's name or identity.

automation: The process of making something operate automatically.

budget: The amount of money available or required for a particular purpose.

freelancer: A person who works on their own—by the hour, day, or job—rather than on a regular basis for a single employer.

intercept: To cut off from an intended destination.

manufacture: The making of goods by manual labor or machinery, especially on a large scale.

peers: People who are equal to one another in age, background, or social status.

precision: The quality or state of being exact.

prejudice: Unreasonable and hostile feelings or opinions regarding a religious, ethnic, racial, or social group.

replicate: To produce an exact copy.

surveying: The scientific method of determining the exact form, boundaries, or position of a piece of land.

INDEX

WEBSITES

Due to the changing nature of Internet links, PowerKids Press has developed an online list of websites related to the subject of this book. This site is updated regularly. Please use this link to access the list: www.powerkidslinks.com/eccs/posneg